THE
ABUNDANCE
MIND-SET

Also by Joel Osteen

ALL THINGS ARE WORKING FOR
   YOUR GOOD
*Daily Readings from All Things Are
   Working for Your Good*

BLESSED IN THE DARKNESS
Blessed in the Darkness Journal
Blessed in the Darkness Study Guide

BREAK OUT!
Break Out! Journal
Daily Readings from Break Out!

EVERY DAY A FRIDAY
Every Day a Friday Journal
*Daily Readings from Every Day
   a Friday*

FRESH START
Fresh Start Study Guide

I DECLARE
I Declare Personal Application Guide

NEXT LEVEL THINKING
Next Level Thinking Study Guide
*Daily Readings from Next Level
   Thinking*

THE POWER OF I AM
The Power of I Am Journal
The Power of I Am Study Guide
*Daily Readings from The Power of
   I Am*

THINK BETTER, LIVE BETTER

Think Better, Live Better Journal
Think Better, Live Better Study Guide
*Daily Readings from Think Better,
   Live Better*

*Two Words That Will Change
   Your Life Today*

WITH VICTORIA OSTEEN
Our Best Life Together
Wake Up to Hope Devotional

YOU CAN, YOU WILL
You Can, You Will Journal
*Daily Readings from You Can,
   You Will*

YOUR BEST LIFE NOW
Your Best Life Begins Each Morning
Your Best Life Now for Moms
Your Best Life Now Journal
Your Best Life Now Study Guide
*Daily Readings from Your Best
   Life Now*
*Scriptures and Meditations for
   Your Best Life Now*
Starting Your Best Life Now

THE
ABUNDANCE
MIND-SET

SUCCESS STARTS HERE

JOEL OSTEEN

New York • Nashville

FaithWords
Hachette Book Group
1290 Avenue of the Americas
New York, NY 10104
faithwords.com
twitter.com/faithwords

First Edition: June 2020

FaithWords is a division of Hachette Book Group, Inc. The FaithWords name
and logo are trademarks of Hachette Book Group, Inc.

The publisher is not responsible for websites (or their content) that are not
owned by the publisher.

The Hachette Speakers Bureau provides a wide range of authors for speaking
events. To find out more, go to www.hachettespeakersbureau.com or call
(866) 376-6591.

Literary development: Lance Wubbels Literary Services, Bloomington,
Minnesota.

Print book interior design by Bart Dawson.

Library of Congress Control Number: 2020932495

ISBN: 978-1-5460-3869-6 (hardcover), 978-1-5460-3868-9 (ebook)

Printed in the United States of America
LSC-C
10 9 8 7 6 5 4 3 2

CONTENTS

INTRODUCTION

We all have vision. Every one of us has a picture in our mind of our self, our family, our future. The question is: What does your picture look like? Do you see yourself rising higher, overcoming obstacles, and living an abundant life? Or do you have a picture of yourself struggling, defeated, addicted, overweight, and never getting good breaks? The pictures you allow in your mind will determine what kind of life you live. If your vision is limited, your life will be limited. The Scripture says that as a man thinks, so is he.

Before your dream can come to pass, you have to see yourself accomplishing that dream. You have to get a picture of it. Before you get the promotion or break the addiction, you have to see it happening in your imagination. The pictures you keep in front of you—your vision—not only drops down into your spirit but it gets into your subconscious mind. Once something is in the subconscious, it will pull you toward it like gravity without you even thinking about it.

Many people have negative images in their subconscious mind. They see themselves weak, defeated, inferior, and wonder why it feels like something is always pulling against them. It's always a struggle. They never feel good about themselves. It's because they have the wrong images. If you will change those pictures and start seeing yourself the way God sees you—blessed, prosperous, healthy, strong, talented, successful—instead of having something pulling against you, it will be pulling for you. You'll be moving toward blessing, favor, promotion, and abundance.

The Scripture says, "Where there is no vision, the people perish." It doesn't say where there is no money, no opportunity, or no talent. What limits us is a lack of vision. Dare to dream again. Dare to have a big vision for an abundant life, and trust God to bring it to pass. You don't have to figure out how it's going to happen. All you have to do is believe. One touch of God's favor can bring any dream to pass. But you've got to see it on the inside before it will ever come to pass on the outside.

As you read these pages, I'll help you get an abundant mind-set for your life, and one day soon instead of just having a dream, you'll be living the dream. Your vision will become reality.

CHAPTER ONE

HAVE AN ABUNDANT MIND-SET

God's dream for your life is that you would be blessed in such a way that you could be a blessing to others. David said, "My cup runs over." God is an overflow God. But here's the key: You can't go around thinking thoughts of lack, not enough, struggle, and expect to have abundance. If you've been under pressure for a long time and have difficulty making ends meet, it's easy to develop a limited mind-set. *I'll never get out of this neighborhood.* Or, *I'll never have enough to send my kids to college.* That may be where you are now, but that's not where you have to stay.

God is called El Shaddai, the God of More Than Enough. Not the God of Barely Enough or the God of Just Help Me Make It Through. He's the God of Overflow. The God of Abundance.

Psalm 35 says, "Let them say continually, 'Let the Lord be magnified who takes pleasure in the prosperity of His children.'" They were supposed to go around constantly saying, "God takes pleasure in prospering me." It was to help them develop this abundant mind-set. Your life is moving toward what you're constantly thinking about. If you're always thinking thoughts of lack, not enough, and struggle, you're moving toward the wrong things. All through the day, meditate on these thoughts: overflow, abundance, God takes pleasure in prospering me.

BARELY ENOUGH, JUST ENOUGH, AND MORE THAN ENOUGH

In the Scripture, the Israelites had been in slavery for many years. That was the land of Barely Enough. They were just enduring, surviving, barely making it through. One day God brought them out of slavery and took them into the desert. That was the land of Just Enough. Their needs were supplied, but nothing extra. It says their clothes didn't wear out for forty years. I'm sure they were grateful. I don't know about you, but I don't particularly want to wear these same clothes for the next forty years. If I have to, I'm not going to complain, but that's not my idea of abundance. It wasn't God's either. God eventually took them into the Promised Land. That was the land of More Than Enough. The food and supplies were plenteous. The bundles of grapes were so large that two grown men had to carry them. It's called "the land flowing with milk and honey." *Flowing* means it didn't stop. It never ran out. It continued to have an abundance. That's where God is taking you.

You may be in the land of Barely Enough right now. You don't know how you're going to make it through next week. Don't worry. God hasn't forgotten about you. God clothes the lilies of the field. He feeds the birds of the air. He is going to take care of you.

You may be in the land of Just Enough. Your needs are supplied. You're grateful, but there's nothing extra, nothing to accomplish your dreams. God is saying, "I did not breathe My life into you to live in the land of Barely Enough. I didn't create you to live in the land of Just Enough." Those are seasons. Those are tests. But they are not permanent. Don't put your stakes down. You are passing through. It is only temporary. God has a Promised Land for you. He has a place of abundance, of more than enough, where it's flowing with provision, not just one time, but you'll continue to increase. You will continue to have plenty.

If you're in the land of Barely Enough, don't you dare settle there. That is where you are; it is not who you are. That is your location; it's not your identity. You are a child of the Most High God. No matter what it looks like, have this abundant mind-set. Keep reminding yourself, "God takes pleasure in prospering me. I am the head and never the tail."

The Scripture says God will supply our needs "according to His riches." So often we look at our situations and think, *I'll never get ahead. Business is slow,* or *I'm in the projects. I'll never get out.* But it's not according to what you have; it's according to what He has. The good news is God owns it all. One touch of God's favor can blast you out of Barely Enough and put you into More Than Enough. God has ways to increase you beyond your normal income, beyond your salary, beyond what's predictable. Quit telling yourself, "This is all I'll ever have. Granddaddy was broke. Momma and Daddy didn't have anything. My dog is on welfare. My cat is homeless." Let go of all of that and have an abundant mentality. "This is not where I'm staying. I am blessed. I am prosperous. I am headed to overflow, to the land of More Than Enough."

SKINNY GOAT OR
FATTED CALF

I received a letter from a young couple. They had
both been raised in low-income families. All they
saw modeled growing up was lack, struggle, can't
get ahead. Their families had accepted it, but not
this couple. They had been coming to Lakewood
and didn't have a not-enough mentality. They had
an abundant mentality. They knew God had a
Promised Land in store for them. They took a step
of faith. On very average incomes, they decided to
build their own house. They didn't take out a loan.
Whenever they had extra funds, they would buy the
materials and hire the contractors. A couple of years
later, they moved into a beautiful house in a nice
neighborhood, all debt free. It was as though God
had multiplied their funds. Not long ago they sold
that house for twice what they had put into it. The
lady wrote, "We never dreamed we would be blessed
like we are today." She went on to say, "My great-
grandparents and my grandparents always told me
that if I had beans and rice, that was good enough.
But I always knew one day I would have steak."

If you're going to become everything God has created you to be, you have to make up your mind as she did. You are not going to settle for beans and rice. You are not going to get stuck in the land of Barely Enough or the land of Just Enough, but you're going to keep praying, believing, expecting, hoping, dreaming, working, and being faithful until you make it all the way into the land of More Than Enough. Now, there is nothing wrong with beans and rice. Nothing wrong with surviving. But God wants you to go further. God wants you to set a new standard for your family. He is an overflow God, a more-than-enough God.

Jesus told a parable about a prodigal son. This young man left home and blew all of his money, wasted his inheritance, and decided to return home. When his father saw him—the father represents God—he said to the staff, "Go kill the fatted calf. We're going to have a party."

But the older brother got upset. He said, "Dad, I've been with you this whole time, and you've never even given me a skinny goat."

Let me ask you. Do you have a fatted-calf

mentality, or do you have a skinny-goat mentality? Do you think beans and rice are good enough, or do you say, "I want some enchiladas. I want some fajitas. I want some sopaipillas"? You can live on bread and water. You can survive in the land of Barely Enough. We can endure the land of Just Enough. "Just enough to make it through. Just enough to pay my bills this week." But that is not God's best. Your heavenly Father, the One who breathed life into you, is saying, "I have a fatted calf for you. I have a place for you in the land of More Than Enough."

Now don't go around thinking that you'll never get ahead. You'll never live in a nice place. You'll never have enough to accomplish your dreams. Get rid of that skinny-goat mentality and start having a fatted-calf mentality. God wants you to overflow with His goodness. He has ways to increase you that you've never dreamed.

ONE TOUCH OF GOD'S FAVOR

I received a letter from a single mother. She immigrated to the United States from Europe many years ago. English is not her first language. She had three small children and didn't know how she would ever be able to afford to send them to college. It seemed as though she was at a disadvantage, living in a foreign country all alone, not knowing anybody.

She applied for a job as a secretary at a prestigious university. Several dozen other people applied for the same position. When she saw all the competition, she was tempted to feel intimidated. Negative thoughts were bombarding her mind. To make matters worse, the lady conducting the interview was harsh and condescending. But this mother didn't get frustrated. She didn't have an underdog mentality, thinking, *What's the use? I'm at a disadvantage. I'll never get ahead.* She had a fatted-calf mentality. She didn't see a way, but she knew God had a way.

All the applicants had to take a five-minute typing test. She was not a fast typist, but she started typing, doing her best. The bell went off signaling that her five minutes were up, so she stopped typing. But the lady in charge had gotten distracted answering a phone call and said to her gruffly, "Keep typing! That's not your bell." But it was her bell. It was right in front of her. She said, "Okay," and typed another five minutes. They added up the number of words she typed—ten minutes' worth—and divided it by five, and by far she had the best typing skills and ended up getting the job. One of the benefits of working for this university is that your children get to go to school for free. That was over thirty years ago. Today, all three of her children have graduated from this very prestigious university, receiving over seven hundred thousand dollars in education all free of charge.

One touch of God's favor can thrust you into more than enough. Don't talk yourself out of it. All through the day, say, "I am prosperous. I am coming into overflow. I will lend and not borrow."

A PLACE OF ABUNDANCE

When the Israelites were in the desert in the land of Just Enough, they got tired of eating the same thing every day. They said, "Moses, we want some meat to eat out here." They were complaining, but at least for a little while they had a fatted-calf mentality.

Moses thought, *That's impossible. Meat out here in the desert? Steak for two million people?* There were no grocery stores, no warehouses to buy truckloads of meat. But God has ways to increase you that you've never thought of. God simply shifted the direction of the wind and caused a huge flock of quail to come into the camp. They didn't have to go after it. The food came to them. What's interesting is that quail don't normally travel that far away from the water. If there had not been a strong wind, the quail would have never made it way out there in the desert. What am I saying? God knows how to get your provision to you.

A statistician ran some numbers. Based on the size of the camp, the number of people, and enough quail to be three feet off the ground as the Scripture says, he concluded that there were approximately 105 million quail that came into the camp. That's an abundant God. He could have given them a couple of quail per person, which would have been four or five million quail. But God doesn't just want to meet your needs; He wants to do it in abundance. The question is, are you thinking skinny goat or are you thinking fatted calf?

"Well, Joel. I could never afford a nice place to live." Can I say this respectfully? Skinny goat.

"I could never send my kids to the college they really want to attend." Skinny goat.

"I could never build that orphanage. I could never support other families. I can barely support my own family."

Friend, God has a fatted calf, a place of abundance for you. He is not limited by your circumstances, by how you were raised, or by what you don't have. He is limited by what you're believing. Maybe you've had that skinny goat with you for years and years. You've become best friends. You need to announce to him today, "I'm sorry, but our relationship is over. It's done. We're going to be parting ways."

He may cry and complain, "Baa-ah." He may ask, "Is there someone else?"

Tell him, "Yes, I've found a fatted calf. No more thinking not enough, barely enough, just enough. From now on I'm thinking more than enough; an abundant mind-set."

PRESSED DOWN AND RUNNING OVER

When you live with this attitude, God will bless you in ways you've never imagined. I talked to a lady who has been through a lot of struggles. For years she was barely making it, but every Sunday she and her two sons would be here at Lakewood. In spite of all the obstacles, they didn't have a skinny-goat mentality. There were in the land of Barely Enough, but they didn't put their stakes down. They knew that wasn't their permanent address.

As this mother was, you have to be faithful in the wilderness if you're going to make it into the Promised Land. I'm not saying that everything is going to change overnight. There are going to be seasons of testing and proving. Thoughts are going to tell you, *It's never going to change,* but don't believe those lies. Keep being faithful right where you are, honoring God, thanking Him that you're coming into overflow.

This lady's son, from the time he was a little boy, always said that he was going to get a scholarship to go to college. He could have thought, *We're poor. I'm at a disadvantage.* But this mother taught her sons that God is a God of abundance. A while back, her son graduated number two in his high school. He received not one scholarship, not two, not seven. He was awarded nine scholarships, totaling more than 1.3 million dollars! His undergraduate, his master's, and his doctorate degrees are all paid for at Georgetown University. That's what happens when you say good-bye to the skinny goat and hello to the fatted calf.

Jesus talked about how when we give, it will be given back to us as good measure, pressed down, shaken together, and running over. What does that mean, *pressed down*?

I used to make chocolate chip cookies with our children. The recipe calls for three-fourths of a cup of brown sugar. When you pour the brown sugar in, it's so thick and dense, even when it hits the mark for three-fourths, you have to press it down. When you do, you can put in about twice what it looked like initially.

That's what God is saying. When you look full, you think you're blessed and healthy. All you need is one scholarship. You just want the house to sell for what you put into it. You just want quail for a day or two. God says, "That's fine, but I'm an over-flow God. I'm a more-than-enough God. I'm about to press it down and make room for more of My increase. I'm going to press it down and show you My favor in a new way."

After He presses it down, He is going to shake it together and not just fill it to the top. He is going to take it one step further and give you so much that you're running over. You just wanted one scholar-ship. God says, "That's fine. I'm going to give you nine to make sure you're covered." You just wanted to get your money out of the house. God says, "I'm going to cause it to sell for double." You just wanted quail for a day or two. God says, "I'm going to give you steak for a whole month." That's the way our God is. Why don't you get in agreement and say, "God, I'm ready. I'm a giver. I have an abundant mentality. Lord, I want to thank You for good measure, pressed down, shaken together, and running over in my life."

OUT OF LACK INTO A GOOD AND SPACIOUS LAND

A friend of mine has a son who got his driver's license a while back and really wanted a car. His father said to him, "Let's believe that God will give you a car." The son replied, "Dad, God is not going to give me a car. You can buy me a car." He said, "No, let's pray." They asked God to somehow make a way that he could have a car. A couple of months later, this man's employer called him in and said, "For the last two years, we've made a mistake on your paycheck. We've been underpaying you." They handed him a check for five hundred dollars more than the car they had been hoping to buy.

The Scripture says, "Is there anything too hard for the Lord?" There is no telling what God will do if you'll get rid of the skinny goat. God is about to press some things down. He is about to make room to show you His increase in a new way.

It says in the book of Exodus, "I am bringing you out of lack into a good and spacious land." Not a small land. Not a little place. Tight. Crowded. Not enough room. Receive this into your spirit. God is bringing you into a spacious land. A land of more than enough. A land of plenty of room. A land that's flowing with increase, flowing with good breaks, flowing with opportunity, where you not only have enough for yourself, but you're running over. Running over with space. Running over with supplies. Running over with opportunity. If you're not in a good and spacious place, my challenge is, don't settle there. Don't let the skinny-goat mentality take root. Don't think beans and rice is good enough. That is not your permanent address. It's only temporary. God is taking you to a good and a spacious land.

"Well, Joel," you say, "are you one of those prosperity ministers?"

I don't like that term. That's somebody who talks only about finances. Prosperity to me is having your health. It's having peace in your mind. It's being able to sleep at night. Having good relationships. There are many things that money cannot buy. While I don't like the term *prosperity minister*, I must say I am not a poverty minister. I can't find a single verse in the Scripture that suggests we are supposed to drag around not having enough, not able to afford what we want, living off the leftovers, in the land of Not Enough. We were created to be the head and not the tail. Jesus came that we might live an abundant life. We represent Almighty God here on this earth. We should be examples of His goodness—so blessed, so prosperous, so generous, so full of joy—that other people want what we have.

If I brought my two children into your house and their clothes were all raggedy and worn out, with holes in their shoes, and their hair not combed, you would look at me and think, *What kind of father is he?* It would be a poor reflection on me. When you look good, dress well, live in a nice place, excel in your career, and are generous with others, that brings a smile to God's face. It brings Him pleasure to prosper you.

THE POWER TO GET WEALTH

My father was raised during the Great Depression. He grew up extremely poor and developed a poverty mind-set. He was taught in seminary that you had to be poor to show God that you were holy. The church he pastored made sure he stayed holy by keeping him poor. He was making a little over one hundred dollars a week, trying to raise his children, barely surviving. One time he and my mom kept a guest minister in their home all week. Sunday after the service, a businessman came up to my father and handed him a check for a thousand dollars. That's like five thousand dollars today. He said, "I want you to have this personally to help take care of the expenses of the guest minister." My father took the check by its corner as though it was contaminated. He said, "Oh, no, I could never receive this. We must put it in the church offering." He walked toward the offering plate, and with every step something said, "Don't do it. Receive God's blessings. Receive God's favor." He ignored it and dropped it in the offering plate. When he did, he said he felt sick to his stomach.

There is something inside us that says we're supposed to be blessed. We're supposed to live an abundant life. It's because we are children of the King. It was put there by our Creator. But here's the key: You have to give God permission to prosper you. You can't go around with a lack mentality, thinking, *I'll just take the leftovers to show everyone how humble I am. After all, God wouldn't want me to have too much. That would be greedy. That would be selfish.* Get rid of that false sense of humility. That's going to keep you from an abundant life.

Consider these words from Deuteronomy 28 in *The Message* translation: "God will lavish you with good things. He will throw open the doors of His sky vaults and rain down favor. You will always be the top dog and never the bottom dog." You need to start seeing yourself as the top dog, not living off the leftovers, not able to afford what you want, in the land of Not Enough. Come over to the land of More Than Enough. It starts in your thinking. Give God permission to increase you. Give Him permission to lavish you with good things.

We think, *Is it wrong for me to want to live in a nice house or drive a nice car? Is it wrong to want funds to accomplish my dreams or wrong to want to leave an inheritance for my children?* God is saying, "It's not wrong. I take pleasure in prospering you." If it was wrong to have resources, abundance, and wealth, why would God have chosen to start the new covenant with Abraham? Abraham is called the father of our faith. The Scripture says, "Abraham was extremely rich in livestock and in silver and in gold." He was the Bill Gates of his day. God could have chosen anyone, but He chose Abraham— a man extremely blessed.

David left billions of dollars for his son to build the temple, and yet David is called "a man after God's own heart." Get rid of the thinking that *God wouldn't want me to have too much. That wouldn't be right. That might not look good.* It's just the opposite. When you look good, it makes God look good. When you're blessed, prosperous, and successful, it brings Him honor.

I realize that everything I have comes from God. Whether it is the suit that I'm wearing, my car, my house, or my resources, it's God's goodness. You don't have to apologize for what God has done in your life. Wear your blessings well.

The Scripture says, "It is the Lord who gives you power to get wealth." God wouldn't give you power to do something and then condemn you for doing it. There is nothing wrong with you having money. The key is to not let money have you. Don't let it become the focus of your life. Don't seek that provision. Seek the Provider. Money is simply a tool to accomplish your destiny and to advance His Kingdom.

A THOUSAND TIMES MORE

Victoria and I have big dreams in our hearts. It's going to take millions of dollars to do what's on the inside. These are dreams, not just for ourselves, for a bigger this or a bigger that, but a dream to build orphanages and a dream to build medical clinics. I can't do that with a limited, lacking, "God doesn't want me to have too much" mentality. I realize my Father owns it all. He makes streets out of gold. You are not going to bankrupt heaven by believing for an abundant life. All God has to do is go pick up a chunk of pavement and give it to you. When you have this abundant mind-set and a desire to advance the Kingdom, God will lavish you with good things. He will open up the doors of His sky vaults so that you not only accomplish your dreams, but you can help be a blessing to the world.

My prayer for you is found in Deuteronomy 1:11. It says, "May the Lord God of your fathers increase you a thousand times more than you are." Can you receive that into your spirit? A thousand times more favor. A thousand times more resources. A thousand times more income. Most of the time our thinking goes *TILT! TILT! TILT!* It's because we've been hanging out with that skinny goat too long. It's time to cut him loose. It's time to have a fatted-calf mentality. God is about to press some things down. He is about to make room for more of His increase. Now get up every morning and say, "Lord, I want to thank You that You are opening up Your sky vaults today, raining down favor, and lavishing me with good things. I am prosperous."

If you'll have this abundant mentality, I believe and declare you won't live in the land of Just Enough or the land of Barely Enough, but you're coming into the land of More Than Enough.

CHAPTER TWO

SEE YOURSELF RISING TO NEW LEVELS

One of the most important aspects of seeing ourselves God's way involves developing an abundant, prosperous mind-set. As we've already established, how we see ourselves will make or break us.

Understand, God has already equipped you with everything you need to live a prosperous life. He planted "seeds" inside you filled with possibilities, incredible potential, creative ideas, and dreams. But just because those things are within you doesn't mean they will do you any good. You have to start tapping into them. In other words, you've got to believe beyond a shadow of a doubt that you have what it takes. You must keep in mind that you are a child of the Most High God and you were created for great things. God didn't make you to be average. God created you to excel, and He's given you ability, insight, talent, wisdom, and His supernatural power to do so. You have everything you need right now to fulfill your God-given destiny.

The Bible says that "God has blessed us with every spiritual blessing." Notice, that description is in the past tense. God has already done it. He's already deposited within us everything we need to succeed. Now it's up to us to start acting on what we already possess.

Remember, that is what Abraham had to do. Twenty years before he ever had a child, God spoke to him and said, "Abraham, I have made you the father of many nations."

Abraham could have said, "Who, me? I'm not a father. I don't have any children." Instead, Abraham chose to believe what God said about him. His attitude was: *God, it doesn't seem possible in any natural sense, but I'm not going to doubt Your word. I'm not going to try to figure it out rationally. I'm just going to agree with You. If You say that Sarah and I can have a baby at our age, as outlandish as it may seem, I'm going to believe You.*

Interestingly, God's promise came to Abraham in the past tense, and although it carried a present-tense reality as well as a future fulfillment, God regarded it as if it had already happened. "I have made you a father of many nations." Obviously, God planned to give Abraham a son, but as far as He was concerned, it was already a done deal. Nevertheless, Abraham had a responsibility to trust God and to believe. Sure enough, some twenty years later, Abraham and Sarah had a son, whom they named Isaac.

Similarly, throughout the Bible, God has said great things about you. But those blessings will not happen automatically. You have to do your part, believing that you are blessed, seeing yourself as blessed, acting as though you are blessed. When you do, the promise will become a reality in your life.

For instance, the Bible says, "We are more than conquerors." It doesn't say that we will be more than conquerors when we grow stronger, get older, or achieve some superspiritual level. Scripture says we are more than conquerors *right now*.

"Well, Joel, that couldn't be true in my life," I hear you saying. "I've got so many problems, so many things coming against me. Maybe when I get out of this mess, then I'll be more than a conqueror."

No, God declares you are more than a conqueror right now. If you will start acting like it, talking like it, seeing yourself as more than a conqueror, you will live an abundant and victorious life. You must understand that the price has already been paid for you to have joy, peace, and happiness. That's part of the package that God has made available to you.

DON'T MISS OUT
ON GOD'S BEST

Years ago, long before transatlantic flight was common, a man wanted to travel to the United States from Europe. The man worked hard, saved every extra penny he could, and finally had just enough money to purchase a ticket aboard a cruise ship. The trip at that time required about two or three weeks to cross the ocean. He went out and bought a suitcase and filled it full of cheese and crackers. That's all he could afford.

Once on board, all the other passengers went to the large, ornate dining room to eat their gourmet meals. Meanwhile, the poor man would go over in the corner and eat his cheese and crackers. This went on day after day. He could smell the delicious food being served in the dining room. He heard the other passengers speak of it in glowing terms as they rubbed their bellies and complained about how full they were, and how they would have to go on a diet after this trip. The poor traveler wanted to join the other guests in the dining room, but he had no extra money. Sometimes he'd lie awake at night, dreaming of the sumptuous meals the other guests described.

Toward the end of the trip, another man came up to him and said, "Sir, I can't help but notice that you are always over there eating those cheese and crackers at mealtimes. Why don't you come into the banquet hall and eat with us?"

The traveler's face flushed with embarrassment. "Well, to tell you the truth, I had only enough money to buy the ticket. I don't have any extra money to purchase fancy meals."

The other passenger raised his eyebrows in surprise. He shook his head and said, "Sir, don't you realize the meals are included in the price of the ticket? Your meals have already been paid for!"

When I first heard that story, I couldn't help but think of how many people are similar to that naïve traveler. They are missing out on God's best because they don't realize that the good things in life have already been paid for. They may be on their way to heaven, but they don't know what has been included in the price of their ticket.

Every moment that we go around with that weak worm-of-the-dust mentality, we're eating more cheese and crackers. Every time we shrink back and say, "Well, I can't do it; I don't have what it takes," we're eating more cheese and crackers. Every time we go around full of fear, worry, anxiety, or we are uptight about something, we're over there eating more cheese and crackers. Friend, I don't know about you, but I'm tired of those cheese and crackers! It's time to step up to God's dining table. God has prepared a fabulous banquet for you, complete with every good thing imaginable. And it has already been paid for. God has everything you need there—joy, forgiveness, restoration, peace, healing—whatever you need, it's waiting for you at God's banquet table if you'll pull up your chair and take the place He has prepared for you.

You may have gone through some great disappointments in life or faced some serious setbacks. Welcome to the real world! But you must remember, you are a child of the Most High God. Just because something didn't work out your way or somebody disappointed you, that does not change who you are. If one dream dies, dream another dream. If you get knocked down, get back up and go again. When one door closes, God will always open up a bigger and better door. Hold your head high, and be on the lookout for the new thing that God wants to do in your life. But don't go off in the corner of life and start eating cheese and crackers.

You may have gotten off to a rough start in life. Perhaps you experienced horrible poverty, despair, abuse, or other negative things during your childhood. You may be tempted to let those negative experiences set the course for the rest of your life. But just because you started life that way doesn't mean you have to finish that way. You need to get a fresh vision of what God can do in your life and develop an abundant mind-set.

Maybe you have come from a poor environment, or maybe you don't have a lot of material possessions right now. That's okay; God has good things ahead for you. But let me caution you; don't allow that poverty image to become ingrained inside you. Don't grow accustomed to living with less, doing less, and being less to the point that you eventually sit back and accept it. "We've always been poor. This is the way it's got to be."

No, start looking through eyes of faith, seeing yourself rising to new levels. See yourself prospering, and keep that image in your heart and mind. You may be living in poverty at the moment, but don't ever let poverty live in you.

The Bible says, "God takes pleasure in prospering His children." As His children prosper spiritually, physically, and materially, their increase brings God pleasure. When we go through life with a poverty mentality, it is not glorifying to God. It does not honor His great name. God is not pleased when we drag through life, defeated, depressed, perpetually discouraged by our circumstances. No, God is pleased when we develop an abundant mind-set.

Too often we become satisfied and complacent, accepting whatever comes our way. "I've gone as far as I can go. I'll never get any more promotions. This is just my lot in life."

That's not true! Your "lot in life" is to continually increase. Your lot in life is to be an overcomer, to live prosperously in every area. Quit eating the cheese and crackers and step into the banquet hall. God created you for great things.

What a tragedy it would be to go through life as a child of the King in God's eyes, yet as a lowly pauper in our own eyes. That is precisely what happened to a young man in the Old Testament by the name of Mephibosheth. (I don't know why they couldn't have named him Bob!)

DON'T SETTLE FOR MEDIOCRITY

Mephibosheth was the grandson of King Saul and the son of Jonathan. You may recall that Saul's son, Jonathan, and David were best friends. They actually entered into a covenant relationship, similar to the ancient covenant of being "blood brothers." That means whatever one had, it belonged to the other. If Jonathan needed food, clothing, or money, he could go over to David's house and get whatever he needed. Moreover, in the covenant relationship, if something were to happen to one of these two men, the remaining "brother" would be obligated to take care of the other's family.

King Saul and Jonathan were killed in battle on the same day, and when word got back to the palace, a servant grabbed Mephibosheth, Jonathan's little son, picked him up, and took off running. Going out of Jerusalem in such haste, the servant tripped and fell while carrying the child. Mephibosheth became crippled as a result of the fall. The servant transported Jonathan's son all the way to a city called Lodebar, one of the most poverty-stricken, desolate cities in that entire region. That is where Mephibosheth, grandson of the king, lived almost his entire life. Think about that. He was the grandson of the king, yet he was living in those terrible conditions.

David succeeded Saul as king, and years later, long after Saul and Jonathan were mere memories in the minds of most people, David asked his staff the question, "Is there anyone left from the house of Saul that I could show kindness to for Jonathan's sake?" Remember, that was part of the covenant Jonathan and David had entered: *If something happens to me, you will take care of my family.* But by now, most of Saul's family was dead, and thus David's question.

One of David's staff members replied, "Yes, David. Jonathan has a son who's still alive, but he's crippled. He lives in Lodebar."

David said, "Go get him and bring him to the palace."

When Mephibosheth arrived, he was no doubt fearful. After all, his grandfather had chased David throughout the country trying to kill him. Now that Saul's family had been decimated and was no longer a threat to David, Mephibosheth may have felt that David planned to execute him as well.

But David said to him, "Don't be afraid. I'm going to show kindness to you because of your father, Jonathan. I'm going to give you back all the land that once belonged to your grandfather Saul. And from this day forward, you will eat at my table as though you are one of my sons." David treated Mephibosheth as royalty. After all, he was the grandson of the king. And David was in a covenant relationship with his father.

Mephibosheth's life was transformed in-stantly—that's the good news—but think of all the years that he lived in that dirty city of Lodebar. All the while, he knew he was royalty; beyond that, it was commonly known that David and Jonathan were in a covenant relationship; based on that alone, Mephibosheth knew he had rights. Why didn't he just go into the palace and say, "King David, I'm Jonathan's son. I'm living in poverty down in Lodebar, and I know that I'm made for more than that. I'm here to claim what belongs to me through my father's covenant relationship with you."

Why did Mephibosheth settle for mediocrity? We catch a clue from his initial response to David. When David told him that he was going to take care of him, the Bible says, "Mephibosheth bowed his head low and he said, 'Who am I that you should notice such a dead dog like me?'" Do you see his self-image? He saw himself as defeated, as a loser, as a dead dog. He saw himself as an outcast. Yes, he was the grandson of the king, but his image of himself kept him from receiving the privileges that rightfully belonged to him.

How many times do we do the same thing? Our self-image is so contrary to the way God sees us that we miss out on God's best. God sees us as champions. We see ourselves as dead dogs.

But just as Mephibosheth had to cast off that "dead dog mentality," replacing it with an abundant mind-set, you and I must do something similar. You may have made some mistakes in life, but if you have honestly repented and done your best to do right since then, you no longer have to live with guilt and shame. You may not be everything you want to be. You may be crippled physically, spiritually, or emotionally. That does not change God's covenant with you. You are still a child of the Most High God. He still has great things in store for you. You need to be bold and claim what belongs to you. It brings God no pleasure for you to live in your own personal "Lodebar," in poverty, with low self-esteem, with that dead-dog mentality.

How would you feel if your children had that kind of attitude toward you? Imagine it's dinnertime and you have worked diligently to prepare a delicious dinner. The food is spread out on the table; you are ready to eat. But one of your children comes in with his head down, and he refuses to sit at the table with the family. He crawls around on the ground, waiting for some scraps or crumbs to fall. You'd say, "Son, daughter, what in the world are you doing? Get up here and take your place. I've prepared all this for you. You are a part of the family. You insult me when you act like a dog, begging for scraps."

God is saying something similar: "You are part of the family. Put down the cheese and crackers. Rise up and receive what rightfully belongs to you."

Many years ago, we had two big La-Z-Boy chairs in our bedroom at home. The chairs were delightfully comfortable and, every once in a while when I wanted to watch a ball game, read, or simply be alone to think or pray, I'd go in the bedroom, shut the door, and sink into one of those chairs. It was a great place to just relax.

I came home one day and couldn't find our little boy, Jonathan, anywhere. He was about four years old at the time, so I was concerned. I looked in all the usual places—he wasn't in his bedroom, the playroom, or the kitchen. I even went outside and looked around the garage, but I couldn't find him. I finally went to my bedroom, and I saw the door was closed. When I opened it, there was little Jonathan in my favorite chair. He had his legs propped up, and he was lying back comfortably. He had a bowl of popcorn in one hand and the television remote control in the other. I looked at him and smiled, relieved that I had found him.

Jonathan looked at me and said, "Daddy, this is the life."

I tried not to laugh, but Jonathan's remark made me feel good as a father. I was glad that he felt confident enough to go right into my room and sit in my favorite chair. I was glad he knew he was part of the family and everything I had was his.

Do you want to make your heavenly Father happy? Then start stepping up to the dinner table. Start enjoying His blessings. Put down the cheese and crackers and come into the banquet hall. You don't have to live in guilt and condemnation any longer; you don't have to go through life worried and full of fear. The price has been paid. Your freedom is included in your ticket if you'll just rise up and take your place. Crawl up in your "Daddy's chair" and develop an abundant mind-set, seeing yourself as the royalty God made you to be.

CHAPTER THREE

UPGRADE YOUR EXPECTATIONS

Our expectations set the limits for our lives. If you expect little, you're going to receive little. If you don't anticipate things to get better, then they won't. But if you expect more favor, more good breaks, a promotion, and an increase, then you will see new levels of favor and abundance.

Every morning when you wake up, you should declare, "Something good is going to happen to me today." You have to set the tone at the beginning of each day. Then all through the day you should have this attitude of expectancy.

Like a little child waiting to open a gift, you should be on the lookout, thinking, *I can't wait to see what's going to happen*—not passive, but actively expecting.

Too many people drag around, thinking, *Nothing good ever happens to me*. Instead, start looking for good breaks. Expect to be at the right place at the right time. Expect your dreams to come to pass. Expect to be a winner.

Don't walk into a room anticipating people to not like you. Don't go to the store believing that you won't find what you need. Don't interview for a job assuming not to get it. Your expectation is your faith at work. When you expect good breaks, expect people to like you, or expect to have a great year, then you're releasing your faith. That's what allows good things to happen.

But your expectations work in both directions. If you get up in the morning and expect it to be a lousy day and expect no breaks and expect people to be unfriendly, then you'll draw that in. Your faith is working. The problem is you're using it in the wrong direction.

UPGRADE YOUR EXPECTATIONS

A young person told me he was concerned about taking his final exams. He had studied and prepared, but he was very worried because every time he took an important test, he stressed out and couldn't remember what he had studied. He always ended up doing poorly.

"Joel, would you pray for me, because I know it's going to happen again," he said.

He was already expecting to fail. I shared with him this principle and told him he was anticipating the wrong things. I said, "You've got to change your expectations. All through the day say to yourself: 'I'm going to do great on this test. I'm going to remember everything that I've studied. I'm going to stay calm and in peace.'"

He came back a few weeks later and said that was the best he had ever done on one of his exams.

Let me ask you, what are you expecting? Big things, little things, or nothing at all? It's easy to anticipate the worst. But if you'll switch over into faith and expect the best—to excel, to accomplish your dreams—then you'll draw in blessings and favor.

Some people have had a negative mind-set so long they don't realize they're doing it. It's just natural to them. They assume the worst, and they usually get it. They expect people to be unfriendly, and people usually are.

I know a lady who has been through a lot of negative things in her life, and it was like she was on autopilot. She expected people to hurt her, and they usually did. She expected people to be dishonest, and they usually were. She expected to get laid off from her job, and eventually she did.

Her expectations were drawing in all the negative. One day she learned this principle and she started anticipating different things. She waited for the best instead of the worst. She expected to get good breaks. She expected people to like her. Today it's totally turned around. She's living an abundant life.

You may have had disappointments and unfair situations, but don't make the mistake of living in a negative frame of mind. Instead of expecting more of the same, start expecting it to turn around. Don't think you will barely get by; know that you will excel. Don't expect to be overcome. Expect to be the overcomer.

You may not always feel like it, but when you get up each day you need to remind yourself that you are more than a conqueror. Your greatest victories are still out in front of you. The right people, the right opportunities, the right breaks are already in your future.

Now go out and be excited about the day, expecting things to change in your favor. Your attitude should be: *I'm expecting good breaks, to meet the right people, to see an increase in business, to get my child back on track, and for my health to improve. I'm expecting to be at the right place at the right time.*

DON'T LET NEGATIVE EXPECTATIONS
LIMIT YOUR LIFE

A young man told me: "I don't want to expect too much. That way if it doesn't happen, I won't go to bed all disappointed."

That's no way to live. If you're not expecting increase, promotion, or good breaks, you're not releasing your faith. Faith is what causes God to act. If you expect a break and it doesn't happen, don't go to bed disappointed. Go to bed knowing you're one day closer to seeing it come to pass. Get up the next morning and do it again.

Winners develop this undeniable quality of expecting good things. You can't be in neutral and hope to reach your full potential or have God's best. It's not enough to not expect anything bad; you have to aggressively expect good things. Are you expecting your dreams to come to pass? Do you expect this year will be better than last year? Are you expecting to live a long, healthy, abundant life? Pay attention to what you're expecting. Maybe you have a desire to get married. Don't go around thinking: *I'll never meet anyone. It's been so long, and*

I'm getting too old. Instead, expect to be at the right place at the right time.

Believe that divine connections will come across your path. Believe that the right person will be attracted to you.

"What if I do that and nothing happens?"

What if you do it and something does happen? I can tell you nothing will happen if you don't believe.

David said in the Psalms: "Surely goodness and mercy will follow me all the days of my life." In the past you may have had disappointments and setbacks following you around, but you need to let go of what didn't work out. Let go of every mistake, and let go of every failure.

Expect goodness and mercy to follow you wherever you go. It's good to look back sometimes and just say, "Hey, goodness. Hey, mercy. How are you doing back there?"

Some people don't realize that they're always looking for the next disaster, looking for the next failure, or looking for the next bad break. Change what you're looking for. Start looking for goodness, mercy, favor, increase, and promotion. That's what should be following you around.

One definition of hope is "happy anticipation of something good." If you're anticipating something good, it's going to bring you joy. It will give you enthusiasm. When you're expecting your dreams to come to pass, you'll go out each day with a spring in your step. But if you're not anticipating anything good, then you'll drag through life with no passion.

I don't say this arrogantly, but I expect people to like me. Maybe I'm naïve, but if I am, do me a favor and leave me in my ignorance. When I go somewhere, I don't have all these walls up. I'm not defensive, insecure, intimidated, or thinking, *They're not going to like me. They're probably talking about me right now.*

I expect people to be friendly. I believe that when people turn on my television program they can't turn me off. I think when people see my book in the stores they'll be drawn to it.

I'm talking about having an attitude of expecting good things. You need to get your *expecter* out.

Maybe you haven't used it for six years. You need to start expecting greater things.

There are new mountains to climb and new horizons to explore. Expect to rise higher. Expect to overcome every obstacle. Expect doors to open. Expect favor at work, favor at home, favor at the grocery store, and favor in your relationships.

REMEMBER THE GOOD

When you've been through hurts, disappointments, and failures, you have to guard your mind. Be careful what you allow to play in your thoughts all day. Your memory is very powerful.

You can be driving in your car and remember a tender moment with your child. It may have happened five years ago: a hug, a kiss, or something funny they did. But when you remember the moment, a smile comes to your face. You'll feel the same emotions, the same warmth and joy, just as if it were happening again.

On the other hand, you could be enjoying the day; everything is fine, but then you start remembering some sad event when you weren't treated right or something unfair happened. Before long you'll be sad, discouraged, and without passion.

What made you sad? Dwelling on the wrong memories. What made you happy? Dwelling on the right memories. Research has found that your mind will naturally gravitate toward the negative. One study discovered that positive and negative memories are handled by different parts of the brain. A negative memory takes up more space because there's more to process. As a result, you remember negative events more than positive events.

The study said that a person will remember losing fifty dollars more than he'll remember gaining fifty dollars. The negative effect has a greater impact, carrying more weight than the positive.

I've experienced this myself. I can walk off the platform after speaking and a hundred people might tell me, "Joel, that was great today. I really got something out of it." But I'll be more likely to remember just one person who says, "I didn't understand it. That didn't do anything for me."

In the old days, the negative comment would be all I'd think about. I'd play it over and over in

my mind. That's human nature. That's how negative memories are stored in our brain. The bad takes
up more space than the good.

TUNE INTO
GOOD MEMORIES

Knowing this, you have to be proactive. When
negative memories come back to the movie screen
of the mind, many people pull up a chair, get some
popcorn, and watch it all again. They'll say: "I can't
believe they hurt me, that was so wrong."

Instead, remember this: That's not the only
movie playing. There's another channel that is not
playing back your defeats, your failures, or your
disappointments. This channel features your victories, your accomplishments, and the things you
did right.

The good-memory channel plays back the
times you were promoted, you met the right person, you bought a great house, and your children
were healthy and happy.

Instead of staying on that negative channel,
switch over to your victory channel. You will not

move forward into better days if you're always replaying the negative things that have happened.

We've all been through loss, disappointments, and bad breaks. So those memories will come to mind most often. The good news is you have the remote control. Just because the memory comes up doesn't mean you have to dwell on it. Learn to change the channel.

A couple of years after my father died, I stopped by my mother's house to pick up something. Nobody was home. As I walked through the den, I immediately began to recall the night my father died. He had a heart attack in that very room. I could see him lying on the floor.

By the time I got there on the day he died, the paramedics were shocking him, trying to get his heart to restart. That whole night played out in my mind, and I could feel the same emotions.

Then I did what I'm asking you to do. I said, "No, thanks, I'm not going there. I'm not reliving that night. I'm not feeling those same sad and depressing emotions."

I chose to change the channel. I started remembering all the great times we had together: the times we laughed and had fun, and traveled the world. I focused on the time we went down the Amazon River, and the times my father played with our son, Jonathan.

There was another channel. I just had to switch to it. Do you need to start changing the channel? Are you reliving every hurt, disappointment, and bad break? As long as you're replaying the negative, you will never fully heal. It's like a scab that's starting to get better, but it will only get worse if you pick at it.

Emotional wounds are the same way. If you're always reliving your hurts and watching them on the movie screen of your mind—talking about them, and telling your friends—that's just reopening the wound.

You have to change the channel. When you look back over your life, can you find one good thing that has happened? Can you remember one time where you know it was the hand of God, promoting you, protecting you, and healing you? Switch over to that channel. Get your mind going in a new direction.

A reporter asked me not long ago what my biggest failure has been, my biggest regret. I don't mean to sound arrogant, but I don't remember what my biggest failure was. I don't dwell on that. I'm not watching that channel.

We all make mistakes. We all do things we wish we had done differently. You can learn from your mistakes, but you're not supposed to keep them in the forefront of your mind. You're supposed to remember the things you did right: The times you succeeded. The times you overcame the temptation. The times you were kind to strangers.

Some people are not happy because they remember every mistake they've made since 1927. They've got a running list. Do yourself a big favor and change the channel. Quit dwelling on how you don't measure up and how you just should have been more disciplined, should have stayed in school, or should have spent more time with your children.

You may have fallen down, but focus on the fact that you got back up. You're here today. You may have made a poor choice, but dwell on your good choices. You may have some weaknesses, but remember your strengths. Quit focusing on what's wrong with you and start focusing on what's right with you. You won't ever become all you were created to be if you're against yourself. You have to retrain your mind. Be disciplined about what you dwell on.

Several years ago, I was playing basketball with our son, Jonathan. We've played one-on-one for years. For the first time, he beat me, fair and square, 15–14. I gave him a high five. Then I told him he was grounded!

During the game at one point Jonathan dribbled around me and went up for a shot. I came out of nowhere, timed it just right, and blocked his shot. I swatted the ball away and it went flying into the bushes.

I felt like an NBA star. A couple days later, we went to the gym to play with some friends.

Jonathan said, "Dad, tell everybody what happened the other night."

I said, "Oh, yeah, Jonathan went up for this shot, and I must have been this high in the air and I blocked it, and it was something else."

He said, "No, Dad. I meant tell them how I beat you for the first time!"

What's funny is, I didn't remember my defeat, I remembered my victory. The first thing that came to my mind wasn't that I lost the game to him, but the fact that I did something good. It's because I've trained my mind to remember the right things.

For many people it's just the opposite. They won the game, but they remember all the mistakes they made. They never feel good about themselves. They're always focused on something they didn't do good enough.

It's all in how you train your mind. It depends on what channel you're watching. Don't make the mistake of remembering what you should forget, whether it's your hurts, your disappointments, or your failures. Don't forget what you should remember—your victories, your successes, and the hard times you overcame.

COLLECT THE POSITIVES
IN YOUR PAST

In the Old Testament, God commanded His people to have certain feasts and certain celebrations. One of the main reasons was so they would remember what He had done. Several times a year they would stop what they were doing so everybody could take off. They would celebrate how God brought them out of slavery and how God defeated their enemies and how He protected them. They were required to remember.

In another place it talks about how they put down what they called "memorial stones." These were big stones. Today, we would call them historical markers. The stones reminded them of specific victories. Every time they would go by certain stones they would recall an event. "This stone was for when we were brought out of slavery. This stone is for when our child was healed. This stone is for how God provided for our needs." Having these memorial stones helped them to keep God's deeds fresh in their memories.

In the same way, you should have your own memorial stones. When you look back over your life, you should remember not when you failed, not when you went through a divorce, not when your business went down, not when you lost that loved one, not when the boss did you wrong. That's remembering what you're supposed to forget.

You need to switch over to the other channel. Remember when you met the love of your life, remember when your child was born, remember when you got that new position, remember when the problem suddenly turned around, remember the peace you felt when you lost a loved one.

Remember the strength you had in that difficult time. It looked dark. You didn't think you'd see another happy day again, but God turned it around and gave you joy for mourning, beauty for ashes, and today you're happy, healthy, strong. We should all have our own memorial stones.

My mother recently marked the thirty-seventh anniversary of her victory over cancer. Thirty-seven years ago, the doctors gave her a few weeks to live, but she's still healthy and whole. That's a memorial stone.

Another one for me is December 1, 2003, when Mayor Lee Brown handed us the key to our new church building in Houston. That facility is a memorial stone. I also remember when I walked into a jewelry store and met Victoria for the first time. God answered her prayer. I mean my prayer!

I put up another memorial stone in remembrance of the fact that when my father died, I didn't know how to minister, but God gave me the grace to step up and pastor the church.

That's what I'm constantly remembering—good things. My question to you is: Do you have any memorial stones out? What you remember will have a great impact on what kind of life you live. If you're remembering your failures, your disappointments, and your hurts, that will keep you stuck in a rut.

If you'd just change what you're remembering—start remembering your successes, your victories, and the times you've overcome—that will allow you to step into new levels of favor. You may be in tough times, facing challenges, but when you remember the right things, you won't be saying, "This problem is too big. This sickness is going to be the end of me." Instead, you'll be saying, "God, You did it for me once, and I know You can do it for me again."

This is what David did when he was about to face Goliath, a giant twice his size. He could have focused on how big Goliath was and how Goliath had more experience, more training, and more weapons. All that would have done is discourage him.

The Scripture says, "David remembered that he had killed a lion and a bear with his own hands." What was he doing? Remembering his victories. David could have remembered that his brothers mistreated him and his father disrespected him. There were negative things in his past, just like with all of us. But David understood this principle: Dwelling on defeats, failures, and unfair situations will keep you stuck.

He chose to dwell on his victories, and he rose above that challenge and became who God created him to be. You may feel like you're up against a giant. The way you're going to stay encouraged and the way you will have the faith to overcome is to do like David.

Instead of dwelling on how impossible it is and how you'll never make it, remember your victories all through the day. Get your memorial stones out. "Lord, thank You for that time when all the odds were against me, but You turned it around. God, I remember when You promoted me, vindicated me, made my wrongs right."

Rehearse your victories. Remembering the good things will make you strong.

RELIVE THE JOY

In 2007, a young lady named Rachel Smith won the Miss USA beauty pageant. She's a very bright girl who has traveled the world helping underprivileged children. Later that year, she competed in the Miss Universe pageant. As she was walking out on the stage, during the evening gown competition, she lost her footing on the slick floors and fell flat on her back. Millions of people around the world were watching on television. She was so embarrassed. She got up as quickly as she could and kept a smile on her face. The audience wasn't very forgiving. There were jeers and laughs and boos. It was very humiliating.

In spite of that fall, Rachel made it to the top five. She had to go up and answer a question randomly chosen from a hat. She walked out again to the same spot where she had fallen just a few minutes earlier. She pulled a question out of the hat with millions of people watching. The question was: "If you could relive and redo any moment of your life over again, what moment would that be?"

She had just experienced the most embarrassing moment of her life twenty minutes earlier. How many of us would have said, "I'd like to relive that moment when I fell on this stage. I'd like to do that over again"?

But without missing a beat she said, "If I could relive anything again, I would relive my trip to Africa working with the orphans, seeing their beautiful smiles, feeling their warm hugs."

Instead of reliving a moment of embarrassment, a moment of pain, Rachel chose to replay a moment of joy, where she was making a difference, where she was proud of herself. We all fall down in our lives. We all make mistakes. We all have embarrassing, unfair moments.

You can be sure those images will replay again and again on the movie screen of your mind. You've got to do as Rachel Smith did: Change the channel and put on your victories, put on your successes, put on your accomplishments.

God performed miracle after miracle for the Israelites. He supernaturally brought them out of slavery. He sent all these plagues on their enemies. Even though the Israelites were living next door, the plagues did not affect them. When they came to a dead end at the Red Sea, with Pharaoh and his army chasing them, it might have looked like their lives were all over, but the water parted.

They went through the sea on dry ground. God gave them water out of a rock, and He led them by the cloud by day and the pillar of fire by night. But in spite of all of this they never made it into the Promised Land. Psalm 78 tells why. It says, "They forgot what God had done, they didn't remember the amazing miracles He had shown them and their ancestors."

When you forget what you should be remembering, it can keep you out of your Promised Land. The Israelites became discouraged, started complaining, and asked Moses, "Why did you bring us out here to die in the desert?"

When they faced an enemy, they thought, "We don't have a chance." They already had seen God's goodness in amazing ways. They had seen God do the impossible, but because they forgot about it, they were afraid, worried, and negative. It kept them from their destiny.

GOD CAN DO IT AGAIN

Are you forgetting what God has done for you? Have you let what once was a miracle become ordinary? It doesn't excite you anymore. You don't thank God for it. Look back over your life and remember that God brought you to where you are, big things and small things. You'll know if God did it for you once, He can do it for you again.

You may get discouraged and think, *I don't see how I'll ever get out of this problem. Or I'll never get out of debt. Or I'll never get well.* But when that happens, go back and remember the Red Seas God has parted for you. Remember the enemies He's delivered you from. Remember the battles He's fought, and the restoration, the vindication, and the favor He's shown.

Every one of us can look back and see the hand of God on our lives. God has opened doors that should have never opened for you, just as He did for the Israelites. He's helped you accomplish things you never could have accomplished on your own. He's brought you out of difficulties that you thought you'd never survive. He's protected, promoted, and given you opportunity.

The key to staying encouraged so you can see God open new doors and turn negative situations around is to never forget what He has done. In fact, the Scripture says, "We should tell our children and our grandchildren." We should pass down stories of the goodness of God.

In the Old Testament, we read a lot about the staffs people carried around with them. They weren't just walking sticks or something to keep wild animals away. They were more significant than that.

Back in those days, people were nomadic. They were always on the move. They didn't keep records with papers and computer files like we have today. Instead, they etched records of important events and dates on their walking staffs.

That was their way of keeping personal records. They'd etch notations such as, "On this date we defeated the Amalekites. On this date my son was born. On this date God brought us out of slavery. On this date God gave us water out of the rock."

Their walking staffs provided a record of their history with God. When Moses parted the Red Sea, what did he do? He held up his staff. He was saying, "God, we thank You for all You've done in the past. We remember that You've delivered us time and time again."

Moses was remembering the great things God had done. When David went out to face Goliath, he didn't just take his slingshot. The Scripture says he took his staff. On that staff, no doubt, he had etched, "On this date I killed a lion with my bare hands. On this date I killed a bear. On this date Samuel anointed me as king."

David took his staff to remind him that God had helped him in the past. I can imagine just before he went out to fight, he ran over and read it one more time. That gave him the final boost. His attitude was: *God, You did it for me back then, so I know You can do it for me now.*

Are you facing giants today? Does your problem look too big? Do your dreams seem impossible? You need to get your staff out. Instead of going around discouraged, and thinking it's never going to work out, start dwelling on your victories. Start thinking about how you killed the lion and bear in your own life. Start remembering how far God has brought you.

Rehearse all the times He opened doors, gave you promotions, healed your family members, and put you in the right places with the right people. Don't forget your victories. On a regular basis go back over your memorial stones, and read the victories etched on your staff.

When those negative memories come up, they come to all of us—the things that didn't work out, your hurts, your failures, and your disappointments. Many people mistakenly stay on that channel and they end up stuck in a negative rut and do not expect anything good. Remember, that's not the only channel—get your remote control and switch over to the abundance channel.

Expect breakthroughs. Expect problems to turn around. Expect to rise to new levels. You haven't seen your greatest victories. You haven't accomplished your greatest dreams. There are new mountains to climb, new horizons to explore.

Don't let past disappointments steal your passion. Don't let the way somebody treated you sour you on life. God is still in control. It may not have happened in the past, but it can happen in the future.

Draw a line in the sand and say, "That's it. I'm done with low expectations. I'm not settling for mediocrity. I expect favor, increase, and promotion. I expect blessings to chase me down. I expect this year to be my best year so far."

If you raise your level of expectancy, God will take you places you've never dreamed. He'll open doors no man can shut. He will help you overcome obstacles that looked insurmountable, and you will see His goodness and abundance in amazing ways.

CHAPTER FOUR

TURN UP THE POWER

When you honor God with your life, keeping Him in first place, He puts something on you called *a commanded blessing*. The commanded blessing is like a magnet. It attracts the right people, good breaks, contracts, ideas, resources, and influence. You don't have to go after these things, trying to make something happen in your own strength, your own talent; hoping that life works out. All you have to do is keep honoring God, and the right people will find you. The right opportunities will come across your path. The favor, the wisdom, and the vindication will track you down. Why? You've become a magnet for God's goodness.

The military has what's called a heat-seeking missile. They program a target into the computer and fire the missile off, which can travel thousands of miles. The intended target can be flying in the air, zigzagging here and there, trying to lose it. But it doesn't have a chance. That heat-seeking missile follows it everywhere it goes. It eventually overtakes it and accomplishes its purpose.

In the same way, when you keep God in first place, just like that heat-seeking missile finding a target, God will send blessings that chase you down, favor that overtakes you. Out of nowhere, a good break comes. Suddenly your health improves. Out of the blue, you're able to pay your house off. Unexpectedly, a dream comes to pass. That's not a lucky break. That's not a coincidence. That's the commanded blessing on your life. Like a magnet, you're attracting the goodness of God.

That's what it says in Deuteronomy 28: "When you walk in God's ways, making pleasing Him your highest priority, all these blessings will chase you down and overtake you." One translation says, "You will become a magnet for blessings." That means because you are honoring God, right now, something is attracted to you. Not fear, sickness, depression, or bad breaks. No, like a heat-seeking missile, favor is tracking you down, promotion is headed your way, divine connections are searching you out. You are attracting the goodness of God.

You may be facing an illness. Instead of thinking, *I'm never going to get well. You should see the medical report,* your attitude should be, *Healing is looking for me. Restoration is tracking me down.* If you're struggling in your finances, instead of thinking, *I'll never get out of debt. I'll never accomplish my dreams,* you need to tell yourself, *Abundance is looking for me. Favor is in my future. Good breaks are tracking me down.* If you're single, don't conclude, *I'll never get married. I'm too old. It's been too long.* No, you need to declare, *The right person is looking for me. Divine connections are tracking me down. They're already in my future. Like a magnet, I'm drawing them in.*

KEEP BEING YOUR BEST

When I look back over my life, it is evident that most of the favor and most of the good breaks came to me. I didn't go after them. I was simply being my best, and God did more than I could ask or think. I never thought I could stand up in front of people and minister. I spent seventeen years behind the scenes at Lakewood doing the television production. I'm not bragging, but during those seventeen years, I was faithful. I gave it my all. I made my father look the best I possibly could. I'd go the extra mile to make sure the lighting was perfect, camera angles were just right. I would even go over to my parents' house every Saturday night and pick out a suit and a tie for my father to wear the next day on television. My mother would say, "Joel, Daddy's a grown man. You don't need to come over every week. He can pick out his own clothes." The problem is, I had seen what my father picked out before!

Let's just say he liked a lot of color. I wanted that broadcast to be perfect. I wasn't looking to become Lakewood's senior pastor. I was content where I was behind the scenes. But when my father went to be with the Lord, this opportunity came looking for me. I never planned on doing it; it chased me down.

God's dream for your life is so much bigger than your own. If you will keep being your best right where you are, you will come into favor, promotion, and opportunity bigger than you ever imagined. You won't have to go after it; it will come to you. Like a magnet, you'll draw it in.

When I was in my early twenties, I walked into a jewelry store and met Victoria for the first time. Like a magnet, she couldn't keep her hands off me! (That's my side of the story anyway.) We went out on our first date and had so much fun. It was at the Compaq Center, where we now have our services. The next week she invited me to come to her house and have dinner. We laughed and had a great time. I called her the next day at work to thank her, but she was busy and not able to talk. I called her that evening at home, and she wasn't there. I called her the next day and the next day and the next and the next. But she was always either busy or not available; for some reason she couldn't talk. Finally, I got the message. She's avoiding me. She doesn't want to see me. I thought, *That's fine. I won't call her anymore.* About two weeks later, I was sitting in a little diner eating breakfast early one morning all by myself, and Victoria came walking in. She saw my car out in the parking lot, came and sat at the table, and said, "Joel, I'm so sorry I keep missing all of your calls." She came back to her senses and came looking for me! (Again, that's my side of the story. In reality, she ate breakfast and then made me pay for it.)

Friend, God has the right people in your future. When you honor God, the person He has designed for you, the right one, will come across your path as though drawn by a magnet. You don't have to worry. You don't have to play games and try to convince somebody to like you. If they don't like you, let them go. If they don't celebrate you and see you as a gift, a treasure, as one of a kind, move forward.

Don't hang on to people who are not attracted to you. The right person will not be able to live without you. The one whom God designed for you will think you're the greatest thing in the world. You keep being your best right where you are, honoring God, and God will do for you what He did for me. He'll cause you to be at the right place at the right time. Those divine connections will come across your path.

IT WILL HAPPEN AT
THE EXACT RIGHT TIME

What God has planned for you is much bigger than anything you've ever dreamed. If God were to show you right now where He's taking you—the favor, the promotion, the influence—it would boggle your mind. You may think, as I did, that you're not the most qualified. You don't have the personality or the talent. That's okay. It's not going to happen just because of your talent, your personality, or your hard work. It's going to happen because of the commanded blessing on your life. God's anointing on you is more important than your talent, your education, or what family you come from. You could have less talent, but with the favor of God, you will go further than people who have much more talent. You may not see how this can happen. It doesn't seem possible. But you don't have to figure it out. If you'll just keep being your best right where you are, getting to work on time, doing more than you have to, being a person of excellence and integrity, the right people will find you and the right opportunities will track you down.

Now, don't be frustrated if it doesn't happen on your timetable. You have to pass some tests. You have to prove to God that you'll be faithful right where you are. If you're not faithful in the wilderness, how can God trust you to be faithful in the Promised Land? You have to keep a good attitude when you're not getting your way. You have to be your best when you're not getting any credit. Do the right thing when it's difficult. That's when your character is being developed. If you will pass these tests, you can be certain God will get you to where you're supposed to be. The right people are in your future. So are the right opportunities, the good breaks, the wisdom, the contracts, the houses. God said, "No good thing will He withhold because you walk uprightly."

I've learned that in a split second one touch of God's favor can take you further than you could go in your whole lifetime on your own. Quit thinking, *I'm getting further behind. I'll never accomplish my dreams.* No; God has explosive blessings in your future. He has blessings that will thrust you years and years ahead.

You say, "Joel, this all sounds good. But I don't really have the talent. I don't know the right people. I don't have the money." That's okay; God does. He's already lined up everything you need. There are good breaks right now that have your name on them. There are contracts, buildings, and businesses that have your name on them. There are ideas, inventions, books, movies, and songs that have your name on them. As you keep honoring God, being your best, like that magnet, you're going to draw in what already has your name on it.

When is this going to happen? At the exact right time. If it hasn't happened yet, don't get discouraged. God knows what He's doing. If it would have happened earlier, it wouldn't have been the best time. Just keep being faithful right where you are and keep living with this attitude that something good is coming your way.

When you do that, you're going to draw in like a magnet what already has your name on it. There's healing with your name on it. If you're single, there's a spouse with your name on him or her. If you're believing to have a child, there's a baby with your name on him or her. God has already chosen them to be yours. There's a business with your name on it. There's a number one movie with your name on it. There's an invention that will touch the world with your name on it.

YOUR "EVENTUALLY"S WILL TRACK YOU DOWN

Here's the whole key: You don't have to seek the blessing. Seek God, and the blessings will seek after you. This is where we miss it. Very often, we think, *I have to get this promotion. I have to meet this person.*

I must get my career going faster. And yes, we have to use our talents, be determined, and take steps of faith. But you can stay in peace. You can live at rest, knowing that because you're honoring God, the right people will find you. The right opportunities will track you down.

Proverbs says, "The wealth of the ungodly will eventually find its way into the hands of the righteous for whom it has been laid up." Notice that, because you're the righteous, there's something God has laid up for you. The good news is, at the right time, eventually it's going to find you. That means right now, something's looking for you—not defeat, struggle, lack. You are the righteous. Favor is looking for you. Good breaks are looking for you. Healing is looking for you. Influence is looking for you. You may not have seen it yet, but don't get discouraged. Keep honoring God, and He promises some of these "eventually"s are going to track you down.

Our beautiful facility, the former Compaq Center, is an "eventually." It was laid up for us. It had our name on it, and at the right time, it found us. The building was built back in the early 1970s. It was first called the Summit. Then the name was changed to the Compaq Center. But I believe if you'd peeled back the names when it was built way back then, you would have seen the name "Lakewood Church." God had us in mind when it was built. Eventually, God said, "All right, it's time to hand it over."

In the same way, there are some "eventually"s in your future. The great thing is, you don't have to go after them; just go after God. Keep Him in first place. Live a life of excellence and integrity, and God promises the "eventually"s will find their way into your hands. This is what Jesus said: "Seek first the Kingdom and all these things will be added unto you." Everything you need to fulfill your destiny has already been laid up for you. Now you just have to make pleasing God your highest priority. In other words, before you give in to temptation, be firm and say, "No, I'm going to please God and walk away. I want to fulfill my destiny. I want to come in to my 'eventually's." Before you tell that person off, stop and declare, "No, I'm going to please God and keep my mouth closed." At the office, when they're not treating you right and you feel like slacking off, overcome that attitude and state, "I'm going to please God and keep being my best. I know I'm not working unto people; I'm working unto God." You live like that, and all the forces of darkness cannot keep you from your destiny.

The amazing thing about our church facility is that I didn't go after it; it came to me. Twice, I tried to buy land and build a new sanctuary, but both times, the property was sold out from under us. I thought, *We're stuck. There's no more room. There's no way to grow.* But one day out of the blue, an old friend unexpectedly called and said he wanted to talk to me about something. He said, "Joel, the Houston Rockets basketball team is about to move out of the Compaq Center. That would be a great facility for Lakewood." When he said that, something came alive inside me. I never dreamed we could have something this beautiful or special. It is the premier facility in the fourth largest city in America, and it is on the second busiest freeway in the nation.

As was true for us, the "eventually"s God has lined up for you are going to boggle your mind. It's going to be more than you can ask or think. God has not only already arranged them; He's taken it one step further. He's already put your name on them. They've already been marked as a part of your divine destiny. What's your part? Worry? Struggle? Try to make it happen? Manipulate this person, and maybe they'll do you a favor? No, you don't have to play up to people. You don't have to beg people, hope that they'll throw you a crumb here or there. You are not a beggar; you are a child of the Most High God. You have royal blood flowing through your veins. You are wearing a crown of favor. The Creator of the universe has called you, equipped you, empowered you, and chosen you.

All you have to do is keep honoring God and the blessings will find you. The right people will show up, the ones who want to help you. The good breaks, the businesses, and the contracts will track you down. One phone call, one person whom God has ordained to help you, can change the course of your life. How is this going to happen? Is it just through your talent, your ability, and your hard work? That's part of it, but the main key is by honoring God. That's what puts you in a position for His blessings to overtake you. That's what makes you a magnet for His favor.

DREAM BIG. BELIEVE BIG. PRAY BIG.

I know you are a strong, powerful magnet. You may be very close to attracting that for which you've been praying and believing. You've honored God. You've been faithful. Now God is about to release an "eventually" in your life. It's going to be bigger than you imagined. When you meet that person, they're going to be better for you than you ever dreamed. You waited a long time, but when they show up, you're going to say, "You were well worth the wait."

"Well, Joel, you're just getting my hopes up."
You're right. You can't have faith if you don't first
have hope. It's easy to get stuck in a rut, thinking,
*God has been good to me. I have a good family. I'm
healthy. I'm blessed.* But you haven't seen anything
yet. You haven't scratched the surface of what God
has in store.

Some of you are going to write a book, a movie,
or a song that will touch the world. The idea will
come to you. You don't have to go after it. Some of
you are going to start a business that will become
a global force. Some of you are going to have a
ministry that will shake nations. Some of you will
raise a child who will become a president or a world
leader—a historymaker. The "eventually"s God has
in your future are going to boggle your mind. It's
like nothing you've seen before. God has raised you
up to take new ground for the Kingdom, to go
where others have not gone.

Dream big. Believe big. Pray big. Make room
for God to do something new in your life.

If you would have told me years ago that one
day I would be ministering around the world and

have books translated into different languages, I would have thought, *Not me. I don't have anything to say.* But God knows what He's put in you—the gifts, the talents, the potential. You have seeds of greatness inside you. Doors are going to open that no man can shut. Talent is going to come out of you that you didn't know you had. God is going to connect you with the right people. He will present you with opportunities that will thrust you into a new level of your destiny.

When my father was alive, Victoria and I went to India with him a couple of times a year. One time, we met a young pastor who came from an extremely poor family. They didn't have electricity or running water and lived out in an open field in a little hut that they had built. The man next door was very wealthy. He owned a huge farm with thousands of cattle, many different crops, and he sold milk and vegetables to the village people. But he was greedy and charged more than he should have. Many people couldn't afford it.

One day, about ten of the wealthy farmer's cows got out and came over to the little hut where the pastor and his family lived. Having just one cow was a big deal, because it would provide milk and other products to sell to people. The workers came and retrieved those ten cows, then put them back inside the owner's fence. The next day, the same ten cows got out and came back over. This happened again and again and again. The owner got so frustrated, he told his workers, "Just tell the pastor he can have those ten cows." He gave them to him as a gift!

The pastor was thrilled and started selling milk and other dairy products to the people in the village, but he sold the products for much less. Before long, people were lined up at his door. He was able to buy more cows. His business kept growing so much that the owner of the large farm came over and said, "You're putting me out of business. I can't compete with you. Why don't you take over my company?" The pastor purchased his company for a fraction of its value, and today he has a very successful company with several hundred employees. But it all started when the cows came looking for him and wouldn't go home. What is that? Like a magnet, he attracted the goodness of God.

You don't have to worry about how it's all going to work out. God knows how to have the cows find you. What has your name on it—the real estate, the good breaks, the businesses, the favor—will eventually find its way into your hands. Proverbs says it this way: "Trouble chases sinners, while blessings chase the righteous!" You are the righteous. Right now, favor is chasing you. Promotion is chasing you. Healing is chasing you. Cows might be looking for you! Abundance is coming your way.

TURN UP THE POWER

Don't ever say, "I'll never get out of debt." "I'll never get married." "I'll never be well again." Do you know what that's doing? Demagnetizing your magnet. It's taking away the attraction power.

When I was a little boy, I used to play with a magnet. One day, I discovered the magnet had lost its drawing power. I had left it by something that demagnetized it. It looked the same, but it wouldn't attract anything. In the same way, when we dwell on negative thoughts—*can't do it, not able to, never going to happen*—that is demagnetizing our magnet. You are taking away its power to pull in what belongs to you.

Do you know what I'm doing today? I'm helping you to turn up the power on your magnet. When you realize God has put a commanded blessing on your life, and you go out each day with the attitude that something good is going to happen to you, that's when God can do the exceedingly, abundantly, above and beyond.

Each of us can look back over our life and remember a time when we unexpectedly saw God's favor. You didn't go after it; it came after you. God has done it in the past, and the good news is He's not only going to do it again in the future, but what He's going to show you will make what you've seen pale in comparison. He has explosive blessings coming your way. They are going to thrust you to a level greater than you've imagined. You're going to look back and join me in saying, "How in the world did I get here? I'm not the most qualified or the most talented. I don't have all the experience." You may not, but God does. He knows how to get you to where you're supposed to be. All through the day, make this declaration: "I am blessed."

I believe today the power of your magnet is being turned up. You're about to draw in good breaks, promotion, healing, favor, ideas, contracts, and creativity. God is about to release what already has your name on it. You're not going to have to go after it; abundance is going to come after you. It's going to be bigger than you imagined. It's going to happen sooner than you thought. You're about to step into the fullness of your destiny and become everything God has created you to be.

CHAPTER FIVE

BE SOMEONE'S MIRACLE

Many people are praying for a miracle. They're saying, "God, please send me a friend. God, I need help with these children. I need training. God, I need a good break." We have to realize that we can become the miracle they need. God uses people. He has no hands to heal except through our hands. He has no voice to encourage except through our voice. He has no arms to hug except through our arms. God will bring people across our path so that we can be the answer to their prayer.

You may not realize it, but you are a miracle waiting to happen. Somebody you know is lonely. They're praying for a friend. You're the miracle that they're waiting for. Somebody got a bad medical report. They're worried and praying, "God, please send me a sign. Let me know that You're still in control." You are that sign. A simple phone call to say, "I'm thinking about you. I want to let you know it's all going to work out," and you just became their miracle. Somebody is discouraged, saying, "God, I don't understand this subject. I'm not going to pass this course. God send me somebody." You are that somebody.

Take time to become the miracle. Be aware of who is in your life. They're not there by accident. God put them there on purpose. It's because you are full of miracles. There is healing in you. There is restoration, there's friendship, there are new beginnings. Life is so much more rewarding when you realize you can be the answer to somebody's prayer.

You can lift the fallen. You can restore the broken. You can be kind to a stranger. You can become someone's miracle.

A MIRACLE WAITING TO HAPPEN

My brother, Paul, is a surgeon. He spends a lot of time in Africa operating on needy people way back in the middle of nowhere. It's a remote village, hundreds of miles from the nearest city. The clinic is just a small tin building that barely has electricity, minimal medical supplies, and only one doctor. On a visit several years ago, a young man came into the clinic in the middle of the night who had been gored by an elephant tusk, right through his midsection. Paul took him back to the makeshift operating room to hopefully spare his life. The problem was that there was no blood in the blood supply with which to replenish the man. Paul could have thought, *Too bad. I'd love to help you, but you're going to need several pints of blood. It's just not your lucky day.* Before Paul operated, he took thirty minutes and gave his blood.

He operated on the young man, then replenished the blood the man had lost with his own blood. What was he doing? Becoming a miracle. He could have prayed, "God, he's in bad shape. He needs a miracle." Paul realized, *I am his miracle.*

We all know that God can do great things. We know God can do miracles. But what I want us to see is that He's put miracles in us. We can be the answer to someone's prayers. You can be the good break they're looking for. You can be the help they've been longing to have. It may not be something as dramatic as saving their life. It may be just teaching your coworker the skills you know. Or helping that family that's struggling with the rent. Or taking that young man to baseball practice with your son each week. It's no big deal to you, but it's a miracle to them. It's what will push them toward their destiny.

If we all had the attitude, *I am a miracle waiting to happen*, what kind of world would this be? I've heard it said, "Sometimes we don't need a miracle, we just need one another." Look around at who's in your life. Listen to what they're saying. Is there any way that you can help? Can you put in a good word for them at the office? Do they need a dress for a special occasion and you have a dozen in your closet you're never going to wear? Do they live alone and their family is in another state? You could invite them to have lunch with your family from time to time. Make them feel welcome. Those are opportunities to become their miracle.

"WHEN YOU REFRESH OTHERS..."

A good friend of mine grew up very poor in the projects. He came from a single-parent family, and there wasn't always stability in the home. He loved to read and write, and his dream was to become a television journalist. Against all odds, he got a scholarship to a mostly white Ivy League university. He's African American. His roommate came from a very prestigious, influential family—just the opposite of his family. But these two young men hit it off and became the best of friends. He told his roommate about his desire to become a television journalist. His roommate said, "If you're going to be a journalist, you have to have a better vocabulary. You don't know enough words." Every day, this roommate would get the dictionary out and teach his friend one new word and have him use it in sentences all through the day. This went on for four straight years. What was this roommate doing? Becoming a miracle. He took the time to care. He realized his friend was in his life for a reason. Today, this young man is one of the top journalists in America. He works for a major network and is seen on one of the most prestigious news programs. But I wonder where he would be if his roommate had not taken the time to become a miracle.

"Well," you say, "I don't want to read about being a miracle. I need a miracle." Here's the key: If you will become a miracle, God will always make sure that you have the miracles that you need. As long as you're sowing these seeds, the right people, the right opportunities, and the breaks you need will be in your future. God will get you to where you're supposed to be. That's what it says in Proverbs: "When you refresh others, you will be refreshed." If you want your dream to come to pass, help somebody else's dream come to pass. If you need a miracle, become a miracle. When you take time to invest in others, the seeds you sow will always come back to you.

I met two ladies after a service a few years ago, whom I thought were mother and daughter. But the older lady said, "No, we're not, but she's just like my daughter." She told how before we moved our church from the northeast location of Houston to our new facility, she was very concerned about whether she would be able to continue to come. She's a widow and not comfortable driving the freeways. One day after a service, she was telling a group of friends her dilemma. This young lady, whom she had never met before, overheard what she was saying, stepped up, and said, "How about I'll come pick you up each Sunday and bring you?" The lady was very surprised and looked at her and said, "Are you serious? Where do you live?" They lived thirty minutes apart. But that didn't stop this young lady. She could have thought, *I'd love to help you, but that's a long way, and I'm busy in my career and gas is really high.* Instead, she saw this as an opportunity to become a miracle. Now, every Sunday morning, like clockwork, she pulls up in the older lady's driveway at nine thirty in the morning and brings her to church. After the older lady told me the story, she hugged the young lady and said, "Joel, she's my miracle."

You can't help everyone, but you can help someone. There are people whom God has put in your path who are connected to your destiny. As you help them rise higher, you will rise higher. As you meet their needs, God will meet your needs with abundance. As you become a miracle, God will give you miracles. But just the opposite is true. If we're too busy to help someone else, we're not going to have the help we need. If we're too caught up in our own dreams to invest in others, or too worried about our own problems to encourage somebody else, we're going to get stuck. Reaching your highest potential is dependent on you helping someone else reach their potential. It's like a boomerang. When you help somebody else rise higher, it always comes back to you, and you'll rise higher.

YOU ARE FULL OF MIRACLES

Jesus told a parable in Luke 10 about a man who was walking down a road when he was attacked and beaten by bandits. They left him on the ground, almost dead. In a little while, a priest came by. He saw the man from a distance and thought, *Boy, he's in bad shape. He sure needs a miracle. I'll be praying for him.* He kept on going. Then another man came by, a Levite, or an assistant to the priests, who did a little better. He went over to the man, checked him out, and felt sorry for him. He thought, *This is really unfair. I hope somebody helps him*, and went on down the road.

Then the third man, a Samaritan, came by. Like the first two, he thought, *He sure needs a miracle.* But he took it one step further and said, "You know what? I am his miracle. I'm at the right place at the right time. God put him in my path so I can be a healer, so I can be a restorer, so I can give him a new beginning." The Samaritan went to him, got down on his knees, and began to care for him. He gave him water from his canteen and took off his scarf and bandaged his wounds. The Samaritan then gently lifted him off the ground, placed him on his animal, and helped him mile after mile as they walked to the nearest city. When they got to the local inn, he prepaid the owner and said, "You take care of him. Let him stay as long as he would like. Give him anything that he needs. And I promise that when I come back, I'll pay for any extra expenses."

My question is: Which man are you? It's easy to get so busy and think, *I don't have time to help others. I have my own problems.* Helping others can be the key to seeing your situation turn around. The people you see who need encouragement, who need a ride, who need blood, who need help accomplishing a dream—they are opportunities for you to go to a higher level. When you refresh others, you will be refreshed.

It's interesting that Jesus used a priest as an example in His parable. He couldn't stop. He had to get to the temple. He had his religious duties to fulfill. He didn't have time to bother with this man. After all, if he helped him, he might get his white robe bloody or "unclean." He might not look presentable at the temple. He had all kinds of excuses. But true religion gets dirty. True religion doesn't hide behind stained glass or fancy clothes. It goes to where the needs are.

When you get down low to lift somebody up, in God's eyes, you can't get any higher. The closest thing to the heart of God is helping hurting people. When you take time to restore the broken, you pour the healing oil on their wounds, encouraging them, wiping away their tears, letting them know that there are new beginnings—that's the religion Jesus talked about. True religion doesn't judge people to see if they deserve our help. "Well, she's in need, but I don't think she's living the right kind of life." "He's hurting, but it's his own fault. He's got the addiction. He brought the trouble on himself."

Jesus said, "It's the sick who need the doctor, not the healthy." God didn't call us to judge people;

He called us to heal people. He called us to restore people. He called us to become their miracles. Anybody can find fault. Anybody can be critical and come up with excuses to pass on by. That's easy. But where are the people who will take the time to care? Where are the people who will get down and dirty and help love them back into wholeness?

This third man, the Samaritan, immediately went to the man and started helping him, making a difference. He didn't think twice. He became the miracle. That's the kind of person I want us to be. Not passersby. Not too busy in our career or with church work. Not people like the second man who feels sorry for them but says, "I wish it hadn't happened. I feel bad. I'm going to be praying." Let's become the miracle. God is counting on us. You can lift the fallen. You can heal the hurting. You can be a friend to the lonely. You can help a dream come to pass. You are full of miracles.

POUR OUT THE HEALING OIL

Popular Christian singer Tammy Trent is a friend of mine. She told how she and her husband, Trent, went to a tropical island for a vacation to celebrate their eleventh wedding anniversary. Trent was a very skilled diver who could go underwater without an air tank for six or seven minutes at a time. They arrived at the beach on the first day so excited. Trent jumped in the water and started exploring the underwater caves. Tammy stayed on the beach to enjoy the beautiful scenery. Ten minutes went by, and she didn't see a sign of her husband, which made her a little worried. Twenty minutes, still no sign. Thirty minutes, and she still didn't see Trent. She began to panic and called the authorities. They sent out boats and started looking hour after hour. Unfortunately, they found Trent's lifeless body the next day.

Tammy was not only in shock and totally devastated, but she was in a foreign country, all alone, with nobody she knew. Her parents immediately made flight arrangements to come the next day. The problem is this all happened on September 10, 2001. The next day was 9/11. All flights were grounded. Tammy was there for days by herself, feeling alone and forgotten. She was so numb she couldn't even think straight. She finally was able to pray and said, "God, if You still care, send somebody to help me. God, send somebody to let me know that You are still there."

A few minutes later, there was a knock on her hotel door. It was the housekeeper, an older Jamaican woman. She said, "I don't mean to get in your business, but when I was cleaning the room next door, I couldn't help but hear you crying through the walls, and I was wondering if there is anything that I could pray with you about." Tammy told her what had happened, and the Jamaican housekeeper put her loving arms around Tammy and held her as though she was her own daughter. That moment, thousands of miles from home, Tammy knew that God was still in control. The housekeeper took the time to be a healer. She was sensitive to the needs around her, even hearing the cries from another room. She knew one reason she was here on earth was to help wipe away the tears. That day she poured healing oil on Tammy's wounds. She became a miracle.

SHOW THEM THAT YOU CARE

The Scripture talks about how one day God will wipe away all the tears. There will be no tragedy, no more sickness, no more pain. But in the meantime, God is counting on you and me to wipe away those tears. Are you lifting the fallen? Are you restoring the broken? Are you taking time to help somebody in need? It's great to come to church and celebrate. This is important. We come to be encouraged and filled up and strengthened. But our real assignment begins when we leave the building. Look around and find the discouraged. Listen for the cries for help. You may not hear them with your ears, but you can hear them with your heart. You see when somebody is down. All of a sudden you feel that compassion flowing out to them. You think, *I need to take them out to dinner. I need to go encourage them.* Don't put it off. Don't be a passerby. That's God wanting you to bring healing. There's a tear that needs to be wiped away.

Years ago I went into a restaurant to eat lunch. It was a little diner where you order your food up at the front. As I was walking to the counter, I saw this man sitting at a table by himself. When our eyes met, he nodded at me, and I immediately felt compassion toward him. I knew I was supposed to encourage him in some way. He was dressed in a nice suit and looked well-to-do. I was in my shorts and had our son, Jonathan, with me. He was about two years old at the time. I thought, *I'm not going to go encourage him. He's doing just fine.* I kept putting it off and putting it off.

I ordered our food, and on the way out, since the man had nodded at me, I decided to stop by his table. Just being friendly, I said, "Hello. How's it going?"

He kind of laughed and said, "Not very well. Things are kinda rough."

I didn't think much about it. I just smiled and said, "Well, I know this. It's going to get better."

He thanked me, and I left. That was the extent of the conversation.

A few months later, I received a letter in the mail from him. He told how he was at the lowest point of his life at that time. He was going through a divorce, and his whole world had fallen apart. For months he had been in depression. But he said, "When you made that statement that it's going to get better, it was like something reignited on the inside." That day was a turning point in his life. He came out of the depression. He got his fire back. Today, he is moving forward.

What I want you to see is that I didn't say anything profound. I didn't feel chill bumps when I said it. I simply took time to show him that I cared. We don't realize what we carry. We have the most powerful force in the universe inside us. What may seem ordinary to us, no big deal, becomes extraordinary when God breathes on it. It can be life-giving. A simple act of kindness. A simple hug. Words of encouragement. Letting somebody know that you care. That can be the spark that brings them back to life.

RESCUING HUGS

In 1995, a young lady gave birth to baby twin girls. They were born very prematurely. One of the preemies was diagnosed with a severe heart problem and wasn't expected to live. The hospital's policy was to keep the babies in separate incubators. Several days passed, and the one baby continued to go downhill and was very close to death. One of the nurses felt strongly that the babies should be put in the same incubator as they had been in their mother's womb. After much hard work and much persuasion, she convinced the hospital to make an exception to their policy, and the babies were put in the same incubator side by side. Overnight, somehow the healthy baby managed to put her arm around her little sick sister. Much to everyone's surprise, the little sister's health started to improve. Her temperature came back to normal. Her heart stabilized. Little by little, day after day, she got better and better. Today, both of those young ladies are perfectly healthy. There is a very touching picture of the little baby with her arm around her sister; it's called "The Rescuing Hug."

We don't always see how powerful we really are. God has put healing in you. Your hugs can cause people to get better. Your kind words can put people back on their feet. The Scripture says, "A gentle tongue brings healing." A phone call, giving someone a ride, taking them out to dinner, encouraging them in their dreams—there are miracles in you waiting to happen. Some people just need to know that you believe in them. When you tell them, "You're amazing. You're going to do great things. I'm praying for you," it may seem simple to you, but to the other person it can be life-giving. It can help them blossom into all they were created to be.

One time in the Scripture, Moses was on the top of this big hill watching a battle that was taking place. He was holding his rod up in the air. As long as he had his rod up in the air, the Israelites were winning. But the battle went on hour after hour, and he got tired. Every time he put his hands down, the Amalekites would start to win. Finally, Moses couldn't take it any longer. He was too tired. His brother, Aaron, and a friend named Hur were with Moses on the mountain watching all this take place. They could have prayed, "God, we need a miracle. Keep the Amalekites from defeating us." Instead, they had this attitude: *We can become the miracle.* They got on each side of Moses, and they held his hands in the air. Because they became the miracle, the Israelites won the victory.

There are people God puts in our path who need us to hold up their hands. They're not going to win by themselves. They need your encouragement. They need your rescuing hug. They need to know that you care. They're praying for a miracle. Don't miss the opportunity. Do as Aaron and Hur did and become the miracle.

I saw a report on the news about a young lady named Meghan who was a junior in high school and a star long-distance runner on the track team. At the state track finals, she had already won first place in the sixteen-hundred-meter race. Next, she was competing in the thirty-two-hundred-meter race. As she came around the final curve, about fifty meters from the finish line, she saw the girl in front of her start to wobble, then her knees began to buckle. The girl couldn't run in a straight line and she finally fell to the ground. What happened next made news around the world. Instead of Meghan passing her by, seeing that as an opportunity to beat another runner, Meghan stopped running, went over to the girl, picked her up off the ground, put her arm around her shoulders, and began to carry her toward the finish line.

The people in the stands began to cheer. There wasn't a dry eye in the place. When she got to the finish line, Meghan turned so her opponent could cross the line in front of her. Technically, they should have both been disqualified, because you're not allowed to touch another runner, but the state made an exception and gave them both a finishing time. Meghan said afterward, "Helping her cross that finish line was more satisfying to me than winning the state championship."

YOUR LIGHT WILL BREAK FORTH

It's great to receive a miracle, but there's no greater feeling than to become a miracle. Who are you carrying? Who are you lifting up? Who are you helping to cross that finish line? Your destiny is connected to helping others.

Isaiah put it this way. "When you feed the hungry, when you clothe the naked, when you help those in need, then your light will break forth like the dawn and your healing will quickly come." If you will make it your business to become a miracle, God will make it His business to give you miracles. You will never lack His blessings and abundance.

Friend, you are the answer to somebody's prayer. You can give a rescuing hug this week. You can help a friend cross the finish line. You are the miracle that they're believing for. When you go out each day, have this attitude; *I'm a miracle waiting to happen.* If you will live not thinking about how you can get a miracle, but how you can become a miracle, then just as God promised, your light is going to break forth like the dawn. Your healing, your promotion, and your vindication will quickly come.

ABOUT THE AUTHOR

JOEL OSTEEN is the author of ten *New York Times* bestsellers and the senior pastor of Lakewood Church in Houston. He has been named by numerous publications as one of the most influential Christian leaders in the world. His televised messages are seen by more than 10 million viewers each week in the United States and millions more in 100 nations around the world. He is also the host of Joel Osteen Radio, a 24-hour channel on SiriusXM Satellite Radio channel 128. He resides in Houston with his wife, Victoria, and their children. You can visit his website at www.joelosteen.com and find him on Facebook at www.facebook.com/JoelOsteen.